We Will Not Quit and We Will Succeed!

True accounts and experiences of a family blessed with twin sons born with developmental disabilities

by
Janette Williams-Smith

authorHOUSE®

AuthorHouse™
1663 Liberty Drive, Suite 200
Bloomington, IN 47403
www.authorhouse.com
Phone: 1-800-839-8640

First published by AuthorHouse 5/12/2008

ISBN: 978-1-4343-7979-5 (sc)

Library of Congress Control Number: 2008903035

Printed in the United States of America
Bloomington, Indiana

This book is printed on acid-free paper.

This book is dedicated to my husband, Leroy Smith, and our twin sons, Caleb and Cameron Smith. Thanks for not quitting!

The Smith Family Motto:We Will Not Quit and We Will Succeed!

Acknowledgements

In loving memory of my mother, Katie Mae,
and brother, Phillip Williams

I thank God for giving me the discipline to follow
through on my goals. I am blessed to have a wonderful
group of family and friends who always give me their
unconditional love: my husband, Leroy Smith, who
has always provided me positive feedback toward my
endeavors, along with endless nurturing; the Smith
family…my wonderful in-laws…thanks to Grannie
Edna Smith for keeping us fed and thanks to all of
you for being there to provide the extended love we
need to be complete in our earthly living. I love you
all…Marie, Thelma, Debbie, Pauline, Brenda, Di-
ana, Eddie, Larry, and Bruce.

Special thanks to my sisters and brothers who
always "have my back": Ruby Campbell (Johnny),

Shirley Ann Graham, Maebell Glason (Evert), George Williams, Jr. (Almeda), Leroy Williams (Carolyn), Annette Kennedy (Velton), Mary Ann Dedner, and of course "my twin growing up," Delois Washington. I'll always love you, Sis! My sister-in-law, Almeda Williams, who read my first draft and gave me the essential editing I needed in order to improve my book. My best friend, English teacher Corey Oliver, who has patiently edited many of my works and has been there for me no matter the time of day or night or how many hours it took. Thanks Corey, for being a great "little brother" and giving of your time in spite of your busy schedule. Congratulations on receiving the 2007 Milken Family Foundation National Educator Award. Mrs. Diane Stockman, a very gifted teacher who has taken much time out of her schedule to find out how our sons learn. We love you, Diane, and cannot thank you enough, not only for your time but for the patience and love you extend to our sons. Gwen Allen, with whom I have established a motherly bond. Thanks for listening and pushing me to utilize my God-given gifts. My true friends…Sharon Sims, Eulonda Johnson, Vicki Canady, Miltressa Rainey, Claudette Grayson, Wanda King, and Vernita Wells. I know you'll be there when I need you and I truly appreciate you.

I am grateful for self-published author Ronda Rountree, who inspired me at the Blacks in Government Conference in Nashville, TN (2007). Finally, a heartfelt thanks to the efficient staff at AuthorHouse for helping to make this book a reality.

Now unto him that is able to do exceeding abundantly above all that we ask or think, according to the power that worketh in us.

Ephesians 3:20

Prologue

My husband, Leroy, and I are no different than any other couple. After being married for four years, we made the decision to have children. We did not think of what may go wrong in a pregnancy. We just assumed that our bundle of joy, whether it was a boy or a girl, would be born after nine months, healthy and ready to begin life. Although our pregnancies did not go as planned, we hope that our experiences bring hope and a different perspective to mothers and fathers who did not experience the traditional birth of a child. It is also our hope that parents learn to accept their children for who they are and understand that although it may take those with developmental disabilities or challenging medical conditions longer to master tasks, longer to read fluently, and longer to grasp math concepts, or they may not master certain tasks at all, it is the love and nurturing of loved ones that enable them to excel in their own areas of gifts and talents.

Parents of children with special needs are unique, and we possess what it takes to responsibly raise our children with the ability to be fine human beings without being hindered or embarrassed by their individual characteristics. This will not be easy because we will have to fight for them and defend their dignity for the rest of their lives. We may have to speak up and say, "You can," when others may think they can't. We may have to advocate for services they need when we have been told, "It is not available," or, "They do not need the services." But more importantly, we have to accept our children as they are and nurture them through encouragement and teach them that the only limitations they have are the ones they set for themselves.

Chapter 1

In the Beginning

After our decision to have children and after a miscarriage on December 21, 1996, I prayed to God for twins. Miscarriages are difficult...especially when you want a child, you are planning for a child, and you want what you want when you want it. Miscarriages are difficult...especially when your husband has announced that he wants two children. I prayed to God for twins. It did not matter that I didn't know whether or not twins ran in our families. I had faith that God would give us what he wanted us to have. I had faith that God would give us no more than we could handle. So when our pregnancy was confirmed while I was attending the Air Force Commissioned Officer Training (COT) School at Maxwell Air Force Base, Alabama, in February 1997, I knew

I was pregnant with twins. I definitely knew when I outgrew my military uniforms in a matter of days. We immediately claimed our blessings and we began planning for a life with multiples.

I was humongous by the time I reached six months of pregnancy. I read everything I could find about pregnancy. This was a blessing in itself because the day prior to Caleb and Cameron's birth, I was actually ready to have them since they were on my bladder and I was urinating frequently. It was as if God was answering my prayers as I said them. The preterm labor began with a watery discharge through the night on July 8, 1997. Then, as I dressed for work the morning of July 9, I had a scant bloody discharge. Leroy had already left for work. I sat down on the bed and grabbed my pregnancy book and flipped to the page listing the preterm labor symptoms. I had two of the symptoms. I first called my friend Claudette and told her what I was experiencing. She did what a true friend would do. She assured me that everything would be okay and said that the watery discharge could have been leakage of urine but advised me to call my doctor. I knew something was wrong, though. I had been leaking urine most of my pregnancy, and this discharge was different, a clear watery substance. I then called the medical exchange and had my gynecologist paged. He returned my call, and after listening to what I had to say, told me to lie down and get off my feet. He thought because he had just seen me in the office a few days prior and I did not present with any problems that I was having false labor symptoms. I did as I was told. But then a pain hit me that was unbearable. Now the twins were our first children, and I thought I would not be able to tell when I was in labor, but I was dead wrong. I knew when that pain hit me, it was worse than menstrual cramps, and it had to be what I always heard about…contractions. I called my sister Annette, who agreed that I was having contractions. After all, she is the expert on most issues…or so she thinks. I then called the medical exchange number again. This time I was told that my doctor's office was now open. I didn't care. I did what any upcoming mother would do: I requested that he be paged. He again returned my call. This time I didn't wait for an educated guess as to what was going on with me. I blurted out, "This is your surgery day, and you are in the hospital. Where do you want me to come? I now have three symptoms of preterm labor and I am not going to lose my babies!" I was told to come to the ER. I called my husband and informed him of what was happening and explained that he did not have to come home. My sister would take me to the hospital and my contractions would be stopped and I would return home on bed rest. That is how I had read that it usually happened.

When I arrived to the ER, everyone thought I was ready to deliver. I looked ready, but I let everyone know immediately that I was only six months pregnant. Yes, I heard the oohs and aahs and I knew I had to be seen by the doctor. I still thought that all would be fixed once the doctor stopped my contractions and sent me back home and I went on bed rest. I was rushed to the floor and, after a quick evaluation, was determined to have dilated 3 cm. I was in labor. I was given medication to stop the contractions. The contractions slowed but did not stop. I dilated to 4 cm. I was given spinal anesthesia, and the plan was to attempt a McDonald cerclage. In laymen's terms, they would sew up my vagina in order to keep the boys in longer. However, once I was placed in the dorsal lithotomy position and a good exam was performed, it was noted that the amniotic fluid was leaking. I was brought out of the surgery room. After what seemed like hours, I was told that a cesarean/c-section was necessary. By this time, I knew it was. Remember, I had read "everything." I knew there was no way Caleb and Cameron could survive a vaginal birth. At this time, I had no concept of what prematurity meant. I have a host of nieces and nephews, but none had been premature. What I did know was that my babies were going to live.

On July 10, 1997, we were blessed with the births of twins. Caleb was born first, weighing in at 1 lb., 3 oz, and then Cameron, weighing in at 1 lb., 4 oz. I heard a cry from Caleb as he was lifted up, but that was all. I did not get the opportunity, like most

4

mothers, to hold Caleb and Cameron in my arms. The next day, when I finally saw the boys, I realized the miracles that had occurred. For years, when someone mentioned a preemie baby, I had no idea or could not even imagine what that meant. Caleb and Cameron were our first experience with preemies. I can truly say now that for those who have not experienced a preemie child firsthand, you probably have no idea about the thoughts that went through my mind. I was in amazement. But I never lost faith. My spirit was up and I used the period ahead to prepare for the arrival of my boys at home. Now don't get me wrong; I envy those mothers who have had the traditional post-labor hospital discharge, going home with their baby, but I truly believe that the Lord allows us to endure certain experiences to make us strong and remind us of his power and blessings. Caleb and Cameron were truly in God's hands. They lay in the neonatal unit looking so helpless, covered in Saran wrap. I can recall the long wait we endured while Caleb and Cameron fought to reach two pounds. It was during this time that a pound meant the world. Every ounce counted. They reached the two-pound mark at about two months of age. Caleb was on a respirator for five weeks and Cameron for six weeks. Their treatment included blood transfusions, IV changes, steroid medication, oxygen, hernia repairs, and treatment for infections and viruses, anemia, and stomach distension. Caleb and Cameron's heads had to be shaved in order to make getting to veins for IV placements easier. Our first time holding the boys was when they reached two months of age and the two-pound mark. For those mothers who had a traditional delivery, whether by cesarean or vaginal, and were able to hold their baby immediately, I can only say you were truly blessed. Our wait to hold Caleb and Cameron in our arms was long and trying. If doctors thought Caleb and Cameron were not going to make it, they did not tell us. In spite of it all, Leroy and I were positive throughout our wait. Oh, we were not in denial about the seriousness of our sons' conditions. We just knew that God was on our side. It was during Caleb and Cameron's hospital stay that I learned just how much faith we had. No one could tell us that our bundles of joy would not live. Aggressive treatment is what we asked for and aggressive treatment is what we demanded. I knew that God had our back. The medical staff made mistakes, but none of that mattered. Our prayers went up to God to guide the medical team in treatment. We had to remind ourselves that doctors make educated guesses. They are not omnipotent like our God, so mistakes were inevitable. But when God has a plan, none of that matters.

The toughest period came when Cameron was discharged from the hospital after 4 months, 10 days (November 20, 1997) and Caleb had to remain. Cameron was circumcised on November 19, 1997, prior to his discharge. Miraculously, Cameron came home with no machines or special treatment needs other than his feeding, since his head was not growing along with his stomach. We had to stay overnight at the hospital on two occasions to learn how to get Cameron to eat. Failure to eat could have meant Cameron returning to the hospital and being diagnosed as failure to thrive. Our job as parents was to make sure this didn't happen. Cameron was 4 lbs., 6 oz. at discharge. He was the smallest baby I had ever held. It did not matter, though. Cameron was our baby. Any fear we might have had of caring for him was overtaken by our mission to nurse Cameron to good health. When it is your child, you can find those qualities you need within to do what you have to do. This is what Leroy and I did. Our support and love for each other was tested during these times, and we realized just how much we fortified each other.

Cameron was home on his first Thanksgiving. I say this was the toughest period because our time was spent caring for Cameron at home and visiting Caleb at the hospital. This was where our coordination and time-management skills were enhanced. I had already contacted local agencies (e.g., the Arkansas Department of Human Services Division of Developmental Disabilities Services office for application for the Early Intervention Program, the Social Security Administration office to apply for Supplemental Security Income [SSI], which my sons were eligible for until discharged home, the Women, Infants and Children [WIC] office, the Arkansas Easter Seal Society Infant Monitoring Program, and the Health Department, to name a few). These were services available in the state of Arkansas. What we have learned through our experiences is that there are many services available that may not be known by the larger society. I would encourage any parent with children born with special needs to contact state and local offices similar to those listed above and apply for services. Since many services may not be widely known, you may have to make multiple calls, but don't give up. I assure you the services we have obtained have greatly enhanced Caleb and Cameron's development. And after all, who really suffers if these services are not obtained...the children. As parents, we always remember that it is our responsibility to advocate for our children so that they benefit from and receive needed services. This attitude has helped us to stay focused and determined to do what we need to do to obtain services no matter how time consuming or frustrating it may be.

I had applied for services and was in receipt of them prior to Cameron's discharge. This was important. Taking care of the paperwork and errands were a priority while Caleb and Cameron were hospitalized. Some parents would have chosen to remain at the hospital 24 hours, 7 days a week, but Leroy and I were thinking rationally. We knew that it made no sense to tire ourselves staying at the hospital around the clock and be unprepared for Caleb and Cameron's homecoming. We chose to visit Caleb in the hospital every other day, alternating visits between the two of us.

It was my plan to breast-feed Caleb and Cameron. After their birth, I was prepared to pump my milk with an electric pump, and I did, but only to my disappointment. The boys were unable to digest my milk and instead ended up drinking Nutramigen, a predigested milk. Cameron was able to drink from a bottle. Caleb never sucked a bottle. Due to a narrow nasal passage that caused respiratory distress, Caleb was transferred to Children's Hospital for a brief stay to obtain a gastrostomy tube (G-tube) for feeding.

This surgery was performed on January 14, 1998, and Caleb was circumcised on January 23, 1998.

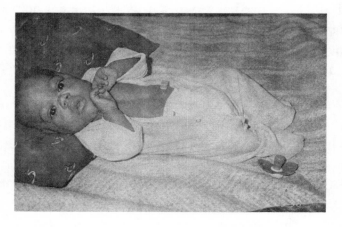

Chapter 2

The Gastrostomy Tube

Caleb had a gastrostomy button/tube (Surgi-tek button to be exact) until the age of 2 years, 4 months, and 27 days. The gastrostomy tube is used to give fluids, nutritional feedings, and medications to individuals who cannot take them by mouth. This was an educational experience for the Smith family. Leroy and I had no prior experience with feeding tubes. We soon learned about cauterizing the site with silver nitrate to remove the dead skin. We witnessed this process firsthand through observation of the Children's Hospital surgery nurse.

One of the barriers to having a gastrostomy tube came when we began planning for my return to work after a four-month leave of absence and Leroy's return to work after a five-week leave of absence. Although we had already decided that Caleb and Cameron would attend a special needs school, Easter Seals of Arkansas A Child's Place Pre-school, the date for acceptance left a four-month period in which an alternative childcare program would be needed. One of our mistakes was placing an ad in the newspaper in search of a nanny for the four-month period. We required a background check, but still did not feel comfortable with many of the applicants who applied. Also, those interviewed felt that a child with a gastrostomy tube needed to be cared for by a nurse in spite of our assurance that this was not the case and in spite of our willingness to train staff on how to feed Caleb through his gastrostomy tube.

We finally settled on a small family daycare, Wee Bear Child Care Center, that in the end proved to be an exceptional facility that provided quality care including gastrostomy tube feedings. After four months at Wee Bear Child Care Center, Caleb and Cameron transitioned to Easter Seals of Arkansas A Child's Place Preschool where they remained until they were school age.

Caleb eventually began eating table food. On December 7, 1999, his gastrostomy tube was removed at Arkansas Children's Hospital Surgery Clinic II. We were informed by the resident that once the bandages around Caleb's stomach/gastrostomy tube site were removed, the leakage would stop and the opening would close. We celebrated this milestone with a gastrostomy-tube-free party at our home on January 1, 2000. Every milestone our sons made was appreciated.

What we actually experienced after the removal of the gastrostomy tube was weeks of leakage from Caleb's site and irritation from bandages. We had to call Children's Hospital surgery nurse to inform of our experiences. On January 5, 2000, four weeks after the removal of the gastrostomy tube, Caleb's tube site was surgically closed.

Our experience with the gastrostomy tube was a challenging event that we can openly share with other parents. We now know that if a child has a gastrostomy tube for over a year, he or she will most likely require surgical closure of the gastrostomy fistula. We encourage parents or caregivers faced with this ordeal to not be afraid to ask questions and be persistent in demanding actions. A lasting affect on Caleb from his gastrostomy tube is the continuous raising of his shirt as if resorting back to his tube-feeding experiences.

Chapter 3

Caleb's Hospital Discharge

We feel that God was preparing us for Caleb's discharge when Cameron came home with few medical needs. This is because Caleb, on the other hand, had numerous medical problems and needs; thus he came home with multiple issues and medical appliances. Caleb not only had a gastrostomy tube, but he was discharged on oxygen and required respiratory treatments and an infant monitor to alert us if his heart stopped beating. Talk about terrified. We took a deep breath and prepared for how our care for Caleb would impact our lives. Leroy built a standing shelf with several compartments to house Caleb's machines and medical supplies. We worked with Easter Seals to obtain physical therapy in the home for both Caleb and Cameron. And most importantly, we listened for the signs that Caleb gave us to let us know when to call a medical professional.

In preparing for Caleb's discharge, we did not wait for hospital personnel to provide services needed. I requested a discharge planning meeting, which included a representative from our insurance company to ensure services/equipment requested were covered, a staff person from a medical durable equipment company to take equipment orders and set up equipment delivery to our home, a nurse manager, nurse, social worker, etc. Prior to both Caleb and Cameron's discharge we completed a CPR class. We were determined to do everything in our power to ensure that our sons lived, and we knew we had favor from God.

Caleb's discharge came with a home health nurse and a blood pressure machine, requiring daily readings and medication. Although the nurse came to our home once a week for a couple of months, Leroy and I provided all the care and treatment for Caleb. We knew the importance of understanding Caleb's condition and health care. We kept Caleb and Cameron in the house for months, with the exception of doctor appointments, for fear of exposing them to additional germs and them getting sick. During the four months of my leave of absence from work and spending day and night with Caleb and Cameron, I gained a newfound respect for mothers, and especially stay-at-home moms. The work involved in caring for children cannot compare to any other job. I now find myself responding to that typical comment I sometimes hear, "Oh, he/she doesn't work. He/she stays at home with the kids." I will take working outside the home any day over caring for children. I actually felt like I was going on vacation when I returned to work.

I am fortunate to have a loving, nurturing husband who experienced this care for children just as I did when he took a leave of absence from work after I returned and stayed at home with the boys for five weeks. I will never forget Leroy's words, "You did well!" No, we did well. The most important component in working and raising children, especially those with special needs, is "teamwork," each individual doing what he/she does best as opposed to performing the typical roles society has defined for us.

Chapter 4

The Christening

Caleb and Cameron were born four months early, surviving when many, including medical professionals, family, and friends, thought they would not. We call them our miracle babies...our blessings from God. With this belief, it was a must that we formally dedicate their lives to God.

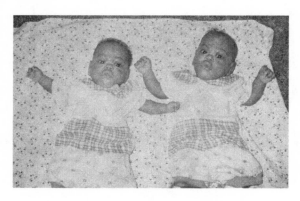

On April 19, 1998, at the age of 9 months, 9 days, Caleb and Cameron were christened at the St. Mark Baptist Church in Little Rock, Arkansas, under Bishop Steven Arnold. We gathered at the 8 a.m. church service among relatives, friends, their grandparents, John and Wanda King, Corey Oliver, Sara Howard, and Stephen Moore, and members of the congregation. Following the church service, a dinner was held at our home, with a photographer on site. This special moment was captured in pictures to remind Caleb and Cameron of the life our God chose to give them. It is our expectation that our sons continue to try to be like Jesus, remembering always… Philippians 4:13: I can do all things through Jesus Christ who strengthens me; and the Smith family motto: *We Will Not Quit and We Will Succeed!*

Chapter 5

A Long Journey

Caleb and Cameron were not typical children who learned to walk, speak up for themselves (i.e., saying, "That's mine," when another child took their toy), ask questions, and jump on their own. For the most part, many of the developmental milestones listed above were mastered with the help of therapists. Having come from a family of ten with 30 nieces and nephews, I have been amazed by the vast difference in the ways in which Caleb and Cameron learn and the help they need. To sum it up, just say that Caleb and Cameron learn differently...but they can learn!

    While in pre-school, beginning at age one, Caleb and Cameron received a wealth of exposure through field trips. We were very impressed and pleased with the varied and numerous field trips A Child's Place Pre-school planned. I can recall that our first field trip to the pumpkin patch was before Caleb and Cameron could walk. It was a wonderful experience for the entire family.

    Learning basic skills proved to be challenging for Caleb and Cameron. To begin with, we had not figured out the deficits that existed as a result of their prematurity. We knew of brain stem damage, but to what extent or what effects this caused were unknown even to the medical professionals. When we were told by doctors prior to their discharge from the hospital that Caleb and Cameron would have some delays but were expected to "catch up" by school age, we expected this to happen. Needless to say, they did not "catch up" by school age. By the time four years had passed, Caleb and Cameron had not mastered colors, numbers to 10, or ABCs. Their pre-school teachers had been teaching a letter a week. Caleb and Cameron had not mastered one letter over a year's time frame. Caleb's favorite color was blue and Cameron's was red. After three years of pre-school, they still did not know colors or, at a minimum, their favorite colors. This was frightening and frustrating, especially since they were in pre-school full-time, received physical, occupational, and speech therapies, participated in the Home Instruction for Parents of Preschool Youngsters (HIPPY) program from age three to five, received Saturday one-on-one academic and recreational services, were read to almost daily by Mom and Dad, were given violin lessons from ages three to five, attended theatrical performances at the Arkansas Arts Center since age two and a half, attended children's symphonies at the Robinson Auditorium beginning at age three, sung in the St. Mark Primary Watson Ensemble Choir beginning at age three, and attended a host of community activities.

We did not need a MD or any other professional to tell us that something was wrong. We initiated a referral to the James L. Dennis Developmental Center, located in Little Rock, Arkansas, with the support of the professionals who worked with Caleb and Cameron. It was determined that both boys were battling Attention Deficit Hyperactivity Disorder (ADHD) and warranted medication. ADHD is a diagnosis the developmental doctor thought was inevitable given Caleb and Cameron's prematurity. How were we as parents supposed to have known this information? We expected Caleb and Cameron to develop and learn as average children would, given the information we obtained from neonatal doctors. I don't know if some doctors are afraid to tell the truth for fear of discouraging parents or if medical professionals just don't know many times where a child might end up or what a child might need. Remember, they are making educated guesses. So, as parents, we knew the ultimate responsibility was on us… to learn Caleb and Cameron's needs and fight for them. After the proper medication adjustments were obtained, we saw a great difference in Caleb and Cameron's educational learning. They mastered colors and numbers and began learning those basic skills that will be needed life long.

With the medications, Caleb and Cameron were learning. Now don't think the first prescribed medication and dosage was effective. I do not want to give that impression at all. Through observation and the help of teachers and therapists, we were able to identify a medication and dosage that was effective for Caleb and Cameron. As parents, we have the responsibility of administering the medication and engaging in ongoing communication with teachers and therapists to ensure that adjustments in medication are made when warranted. As children grow, their bodies change and their dosage and or medication may need to be modified or changed.

In their first year of pre-school, Caleb and Cameron frequently visited the doctor's office. This was partly due to Caleb and Cameron being our first children and having such an extensive medical history. We wanted to ensure their health and safety. If we received a call from the pre-school staff informing that one of the kids was sick, we picked them up and took them both to the pediatrician. We always returned them to school with a doctor's statement. I scheduled a hearing test each year for preventive purposes. If something was wrong, we wanted to know immediately so that treatment could be obtained. In my readings, early intervention was stressed. Caleb and Cameron went to the dentist and optometrist beginning at age two. Our goal as parents is to nurture Caleb and Cameron into strong, healthy, productive men. We are on a mission.

As we became more comfortable with caring for Caleb and Cameron, and as we learned more about their health and what to do in given situations, the medical appointments decreased. Caleb and Cameron still probably go to medical appointments more than the average child, but mainly because many of the services and programs we access require the doctors to complete paperwork within six months of the child attending the program (e.g. camps, horseback riding, etc.).

In Caleb and Cameron's pre-school years, due to the work in physical, speech, and occupational therapy, they went to sleep around 4:30 p.m., soon after returning home from pre-school. They required more than 10 hours of sleep. Needless to say, our home was quiet many evenings. Caleb and Cameron went through a speech disorder phase known as stuttering as well. Cameron began stuttering, and Caleb thereafter began as he imitated Cameron. We learned through their speech therapist and our readings that stuttering is actually common in young children and can resolve on its own. Cameron's stuttering ceased, but Caleb's stuttering worsened. We learned that stuttering can be corrected as well. We requested the implementation of a stuttering program for Caleb. Caleb eventually overcame his stuttering.

A Child's Place Pre-school staff worked diligently with us in our efforts to potty train Caleb and Cameron. This is a task we are still trying to master, and the boys are in the fourth grade as I am writing this book. Many older persons, whom I respect, told me that we should start potty training Caleb and Cameron at age three. Leroy and I set out to do so, although we saw no signs of Caleb and Cameron being ready for potty training. We were very frustrated and agreed wholeheartedly when the therapist informed us that Caleb and Cameron were not ready for potty training. By the age of seven, Caleb and Cameron were potty trained for bowel or the #2 but continued to urinate on themselves well into their fourth-grade year of school. This continued in spite of our initiatives. At age four, we gave them a "potty-trained party." They wanted to see Batman, and Batman they saw. Dad was fully dressed in a Batman suit. Caleb and Cameron were scared and refused to believe it was their daddy in the Batman suit even after Daddy talked in his own voice and took off his mask. The party was a blast, but Caleb and Cameron still did not master potty training.

At the age of nine, Caleb and Cameron were promised a red and white complete football uniform with helmet if only they would master potty training. Now Caleb and Cameron wanted the football uniform and helmet. Needless to say, we saved money that year. Caleb and Cameron did not master potty training. At age 10, we explored psychotherapy. Caleb and Cameron saw a psychologist in hopes of resolving the potty-training issue. It was not effective. It was at this point that we accepted the developmental doctor's reasoning. "Caleb and Cameron will get potty trained when they are ready. They have so many other skills to master that come naturally to most children that going to the restroom is not as important." Talk about frustration! Talk about parents who want their children to excel! Even though the journey has been long, we are still grateful for the accomplishments Caleb and Cameron have made, and we have hope and know that they will master potty training...one day. In Caleb and Cameron's mind, we do know that going to the bathroom to urinate is not as important as going to the bathroom to defecate. They have commented about adult reactions to each. As adults we say a lot when a child defecates on his or herself but may not even know when a child urinates on themselves. In Caleb and Cameron's case, many adults in their school and social environments are not aware that they continue to urinate/wet on themselves.

Chapter 6

Birthdays, Celebrating Each Year

Leroy and I took every opportunity to celebrate our blessings. Caleb and Cameron's birthday celebrations were opportunities for us to thank those who had shared in their milestones and worked diligently to get them where they are today. It was for this reason that we chose to do birthday themes for the first five years of Caleb and Cameron's lives. These birthday parties were usually catered as a thank you to the therapist and teachers.

On their first birthday they were "Touched by Angels." Their birthday party was held the day after their birthday in our home with a host of family and friends. Their second, third, fourth, and fifth birthday parties were held at Arkansas Easter Seals A Child's Place Pre-school.

First birthday party: "Touched by Angels"

Second birthday party: "The Triumphant Twos, Caleb and Cameron Man"

Third birthday party: "Raced into Three as Race Car Drivers"

Fourth birthday party: "Four on the Farm as-Cowboys"

Fifth birthday party: "Fireman Caleb and Cam-eron on the Parade at Five"

Below is a summarization of the blessings we have been allowed to witness and enjoy. We continue to thank God for our miracles and know that the Smith family is truly blessed.

Caleb and Cameron have experienced miraculous years. During their first year of life, they were Touched by Angels as they accomplished great feats. They would then step into the Triumphant Twos with much promise and enthusiasm. They Raced into Three with great determination to overcome all obstacles and gratitude to God for making all such things possible. Then they turned Four on the Farm as Cowboys, roping tasks. Today, "Firemen" Caleb and Cameron are on Parade, blazing new trails in a world filled with opportunities

Leroy & Janette Smith
Blessed Parents

Chapter 7

We Made It to Kindergarten

Caleb and Cameron completed four years of pre-school and were now ready to embark on their experiences in public school. We were excited. Caleb and Cameron were now on medication for Attention Deficit Hyperactivity Disorder (ADHD), but more importantly, they were learning. All was well until I spoke with a special education consultant in my preparation for kindergarten and was told that our challenge for this first year of public school was "to nip the behaviors in the bud." I was also told that "Caleb and Cameron would have to learn how to be students." Now, being a certified special education teacher, I was saying "Okay!" but in my mind I was thinking, "Caleb and Cameron have been in a pre-school environment for four years. They don't need to be taught how to be students; they know." But since I am a planner, Leroy and I met with the special education assistant director and developed a secondary plan just in case Caleb and Cameron did not fare well in the regular kindergarten class.

The first day of school finally came. As we observed Caleb and Cameron on that first day of school at Eastside Elementary in Cabot, Arkansas, we were amazed. It was as if Caleb and Cameron had no clue as to how to be students. The special education consultant had warned us, "Kids like Caleb and Cameron have to learn how to be students." If I had not watched with my own eyes, no one could have convinced me that a child who had been in a pre-school setting for four years had to learn how to be a student. Leroy and I were at the school every day the first week and quickly enacted the secondary plan. Since a holiday was coming up the following Monday, we prepared to move Caleb and Cameron to a self-contained class where they could get more one-on-one instruction. Since we had already identified in pre-school that Caleb and Cameron did better in separate classrooms, and since there was only one of these classes at Westside and Northside elementary schools, the boys went to separate schools. Caleb went to Northside and Cameron to Westside. Imagine being parents and keeping up with two sets of school staff. We managed, and we also knew without a doubt that the self-contained class was what Caleb and Cameron needed. We spent their first kindergarten year working on behaviors and learning how to be students.

Caleb and Cameron repeated kindergarten and the second time around were more mature. They had learned how to be students. In the second kindergarten year they both remained in the self-contained class initially. Cameron eventually went to a regular classroom with resource support but Caleb remained in the self-contained class with a regular classroom assignment for socialization. Over the years, we have placed Caleb in the regular classroom but with no success. We had identified by now some of the differences in Caleb and Cameron's learning styles, which is very important. As parents and adults, we must always be remindful that children with special needs can learn, but they learn differently. One of our biggest tasks as parents is to find out how our children learn, which is not always easy.

We began early in Caleb and Cameron's lives, putting them in various learning environments so that if one environment was not effective, another one would be. To this day, in their fourth-grade year of school, Caleb has difficulty learning in a large classroom environment. We as parents are willing to give our children whatever is needed. This is the mindset that makes life easier. Caleb and Cameron have gone to different schools, been in the same classrooms, been separated in different classrooms, have shared the same homeroom class for socialization, and are now back to separate homeroom class assignments. There is no one way and no correct way in raising children. Every child/person is different with different needs. Our experiences with Caleb and Cameron have given us a new perspective on life and a new perspective when working with children. We as adults, individuals, educators, and human beings must learn to accept others for who they are and focus on their strengths as opposed to weaknesses.

In Caleb and Cameron's younger years, we also had an experience at our church, an environment that is supposed to be supportive, that has stayed with me. This experience stands out to me mainly because it is a prime example of how children gain labels that are not warranted. In a Sunday school class, a teacher continued for several Sundays to tell my husband that Caleb and Cameron were disobedient. This teacher was never specific in her allegations. I discussed this issue with the development doctor and he suggested that we give Caleb and Cameron their Attention Deficit Hyperactivity (ADHD) medication on the weekend since they were usually in educational environments. Until this time, we had been giving the boys the medication only on school days (Monday – Fridays). The next Sunday, Caleb and Cameron went to Sunday school after taking their medication. We received a good behavior report and finally figured out what the teacher's complaint was about. Caleb and Cameron, without their medication, were not children who sat still in a classroom. Children who do not sit still, usually because that is not how they learn, may get labeled as "bad" or "behavior problems." This experience was a rude awakening for us and serves as a reminder of how we as parents must advocate for our children, be careful in our assessments, and explore issues that arise as opposed to taking the word of others. Needless to say, we had no further problems in Sunday school class.

Chapter 8

Look at Us Now!

Our premature babies have mastered so many tasks. It is amazing what children with developmental disabilities can do when we as parents and adults get out of the way and allow them and encourage them. Caleb and Cameron have been diagnosed with cerebral palsy and continue to test mentally retarded on standardized tests. We have read about cerebral palsy and knew early on that it was important for Caleb and Cameron to stay physically active. We started with swimming, the parent-child class, immediately after Caleb had his gastrostomy tube removed, at age three. We initially began with summer swimming lessons but quickly moved to year-round lessons after realizing that Caleb and Cameron were regressing during the school year. They have been swimming year round since age seven and now swim on the Dolphins Swim Team during the year and the Sherwood Sharks Swim Team in the summer. Caleb and Cameron made it to the University of Arkansas at Little Rock (UALR) Meet of the Champs their first two years of swimming with the Sharks (summer of 2006 in free-style competition and 2007 in back-stroke competition).

The Easter Seals Arkansas staff was instrumental in identifying Caleb and Cameron's skills and abilities in the area of basketball. We just made sure we gave them the opportunities to use those skills. Caleb and Cameron began playing basketball their second year of kindergarten. I must say they do have skills in dribbling and shooting the ball. We have experienced the joy of seeing Caleb and Cameron's smiling faces as they wear their basketball uniforms. It did not matter that their first year on the basketball team they did not know the concept of the game and did not listen to the coach much. Of course they had to learn that the coach was in charge and that their plan to throw the ball to each other could not be implemented since they did not always play at the same time. It did not matter that their second year on the team, Caleb still had not mastered the concept of the game, but he took great pride and joy in wearing the uniform. Caleb was fast in running on the court during those first two years, and we took every opportunity to praise him for his running, his strength at that time. I must tell parents that if you missed out on children playing sports, you indeed missed a blessing. I remember thinking as I watched Caleb and Cameron play, "This is what being a parent means—being there, cheering on your children no matter how well they play." Caleb and Cameron continue to play on the First Baptist Church of Cabot, Arkansas, Upward Basketball Team in the winter and enjoy their names being called when they are on the roster for the starting lineup.

Caleb and Cameron enjoy hunting with their father at the deer camp in Fordyce. They were introduced to this sport at age seven when they began accompanying Dad on his weekend deer-hunting outings. They also enjoy fishing and four-wheeler riding. They each have their own Honda 300 four-wheeler that they ride when supervised by Dad.

Caleb and Cameron are involved in the ushering ministry at St. Mark Community Church of Jacksonville under the guidance of Pastor Al Romes. What they enjoy most about this ministry is being able to serve like their dad, who is vice president of the senior ushers and supervisor of the junior ushers. In 2007, Cameron was awarded the title of Junior Usher King at the Southern Usher Regional Conference in Dallas, Texas, after raising $1,003 to be used for junior usher scholarships and activities. This was an accomplishment that Cameron chose to pursue, and we supported him on his decision. We knew that accomplishments of this sort are what motivates children and increases their self-esteem. Cameron was overwhelmed with excitement. He wore a suit for the first time at the banquet held at the Doubletree Hotel in Dallas, Texas, and was escorted in by a teenager. He was "a big boy." He had the opportunity to eat with the usher queen and the usher king and queen contest coordinator, Ms. Gladys Boyd. Cameron did not want to take that suit off that night. We were proud parents who enjoyed the entire event. Both of our sons received attention that evening.

Caleb and Cameron have been attending theatrical performances since age two at the Arkansas Arts Center, Repertory Theater, and Robinson Auditorium. Their active involvement in varied activities leaves little time for them to watch TV. We purposely limited Caleb and Cameron's TV time, knowing that they had much work to do in mastering tasks that come naturally to most children. We also knew that Caleb and Cameron's learning, discipline, and upbringing would be made easier without the added influence of a lot of media.

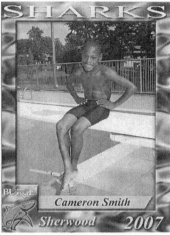

Chapter 9

Staying with the Smith Family Motto

The Smith family motto has always been: *We Will Not Quit and We Will Succeed!* We have ingrained this motto in Caleb and Cameron and refuse to allow them to use their disabilities as an excuse to not reach their full potential. We have high expectations for our sons and see no reason why they cannot accomplish whatever they endeavor. We expect them to attend college and take every opportunity to ensure that they know our expectations and are introduced to the college life. Our job as parents is to ensure that Caleb and Cameron are given opportunities to excel and to thrust them to triumph by allowing them to participate and attend those activities or events that they can learn from, grow from, and mature from. Caleb and Cameron are on a very structured schedule that they maintain year round. This is often needed for children with developmental disabilities and has proven to be effective in our case. They receive tutoring four days a week, attend summer school each summer, and participate in a host of camps. Caleb and Cameron have accomplished great feats. They have much promise, enthusiasm, and determination to accomplish all obstacles. We are grateful to God for giving us the discernment to know that in their time, Caleb and Cameron will master tasks and blaze new trails in a world filled with opportunities. We accept Caleb and Cameron for who they are and thank God for our blessings.

About the Author

Janette Williams-Smith is a social worker for the Veterans Health Administration. She obtained a Masters Degree in Social Work (MSW) from the University of Arkansas at Little Rock. In 1997, she was blessed with premature twin sons, Caleb and Cameron, born at 24 weeks gestation with developmental disabilities. As a staunch advocate for her sons and with an unwavering commitment to her sons' development, Mrs. Williams-Smith constantly seeks and attains services and resources that will benefit them. She takes every opportunity to share her knowledge of services and resources for children with developmental disabilities with other parents in similar circumstances, which inspired her to write *We Will Not Quit and We Will Succeed.* Janette resides in Cabot, Arkansas, with her husband, Leroy, and their twin sons.

Printed in the United States
125613LV00001BB/109-111/P